Poems Momma Never Read Me

elliot m rubin

elliot m rubin

Library of Congress Control Number: 2024921463

ISBN 978-1-962374-30-9 Paperback
ISBN 978-1-962374-31-6 E-Pub

Disclaimer

This book of beat poetry is not intended to be read by prudes, political book-banning conservates, and/or sexually inhibited or repressed small-minded adults.

Published by Prolific Pulse Press LLC
Raleigh North Carolina USA
November 2024
Contact: admin@prolificpulse.com

poems momma never read me

Table of Contents

Dedication

To my grandchildren
Shane, Isabelle, Jonathan, Carter,
Alexandra, Melanie, Mollie, and Madison

In memory of my father

Herman S. Rubin
who wrote poetry and prayers all his life

Preface

I believe poetry is to be read and understood by all, and it needs to be written, for the most part, in plain language for everyone's enjoyment.

Too often, poets write in-depth, penetrating poems where you need to be well-read and/or versed in literary minutia to appreciate the poetry. You will not find this in this book or any of my writings. I try to write so everyone can enjoy a few moments of intellectual satisfaction without consulting a dictionary or encyclopedia all the time.

What is Beat Poetry?

Without going into a deep dissertation, it is basically an anti-establishment form of poetry that started in the 1930s and blossomed from 1950ish to 1970ish.

It is meant to be **honest, gritty, sometimes in a hippy, beatnik style, free from sexual mores and manners, and definitely different from** the Roses are Red, Violets are Blue rhyme and the rigid formula poems most people are familiar with.

Beat Poetry should **irritate** the **uptight, un-woke, conservative-thinking, smallminded people** in America. One English teacher told me that *it qualifies as beat poetry if I can't bring it into my eighth-grade class.*

Enjoy the book.

walking frank o'hara's streets

midtown manhattan's
midnight mayhem
happens too often
when i walk alone
barely dressed women
on street corner's curbs
smile fake smiles
offer to party in a doorway
with a side street slut
who carries a switchblade
or snub nose gun in a pocketbook
and offers
suggestively selected services
for a fee, not for free, and the cop
on the corner suddenly turns blind
after the man in the shadows
in a white floor-length fur coat
tips him cash
to watch traffic jam,
get toasted, not move,
and not the sidewalks of the city
where commerce transpires
between consenting adults
as i, too, turn away
not to be seen
to continue my walk

elliot m rubin

missing friends

i try to remember them
    all of them
harder with age
their faces still appear before me

the boys of youth
    my ball playing pals
who are not now of this earth
yet in reality, really are

i read of their deaths
cannot speak to them now
even if i desired

they're resting

somewhere
while i am still here
alone on a deserted sandlot
as i look to an empty first base
and no one's there
with one foot on the bag and
    a stretched-out glove
    waiting for a thrown ball

instead of cat calls
to opposing batters
the dugout
echoes
an unusual silence

how, i wonder, can i play ball anymore
    even if i still could
i don't remember their names

split open/split up

the opening
on the back of my hospital gown
reminds me of our love
    something is missing

your affection's frigid
like the cold breeze
that blows on my back
and wish it were gone

the strings to tie it together
similar to our marriage
almost complete
so near, almost together
now undone

waiting for the surgeon
to cut out a cancer
like the divorce lawyer
hired
before my hospital admission

elliot m rubin

dining out in manhattan

order a wedge salad
their prime appetizer
sounds fancy
but only lettuce
green iceberg lettuce
with a small cup of dressing
everyone raves about its size
it is a big wedge
but still lettuce
green crisp iceberg lettuce
served on fancy bone china
in a fancy schmancy
five-star restaurant
with heavy, sterling silver forks and knives
but still lettuce
green, crisp, cold, iceberg lettuce
green, crisp, cold, *expensive*, iceberg lettuce
i should have ordered soup

yankee stadium

the boston red sox game
is a popular rivalry
forged in perpetuity —
always a sell-out   stands full,
forty-seven thousand faces
stare down on halogen-lit
green grass, mowed in plaid patterns

top of the ninth
bases loaded, two out,
yankees call in
a newly hired relief pitcher
a former washed-up,
injured, college player,
with tommy-john surgery,
who at thirty-three played
in independent leagues when discovered
after giving up electrical work
for pure love of the game

thousands of spectators
see a mature man on the mound —
in reality, he is mentally fourteen
with a white stitched leather ball
in his hand and a big grin
with every pitch thrown, it's
as if he's on the little league field
of his youth, decades ago,
having fun

matryoshka (russian stacking dolls)

1 - emma's manhattan story

thunderstorms of tears fill her ocean of sorrow
as dark, lonely, midnight manhattan streets
support her with hard, cold concrete slabs,
which buckle over tree roots
to make her journey home perilous,
when unwashed, hungry, homeless men,
who sleep in darkened doorways, eye her passing

in new, red-soled stilettos and a *gucci* handbag
her heartbreak lover gifted her last week
on their one-year anniversary; now their romance
over, trashed and pounded into history, when a
coworker texted her as she ate at *sardis* with her
intended and showed an *only fans* page of a
couple, naked and entangled, with a closeup to
show it was not she in the picture, but another
woman

emma placed the fork down, stood, and reached
across the table to show her phone, to expose a
deep secret not intended for her, ignoring pleas
of forgiveness with an explanation of how her
presents were paid for as an excuse for
infidelity; at the street corner, she called her
high school sweetheart cathy to cry out inner
torment, hoping for soothing words, as she
descended into the train station then stood
close to the edge of the platform, too close, the
train roared out of the tunnel's blackness,
approached as the tall, red-soled *louboutins*
wavered unsteadily from the onrush of air

2 - subway ride

with a whoosh of stagnancy, the subway train
stops, rats scatter beneath the wheels to hide
unseen under the concrete station as her
expensive designer shoes step over wet gum
stuck on the floor beyond the train door and the
handful of riders late at night look up defensively
to see who is getting on, to be relieved it's a
teary-eyed young woman who settles down on a
corner seat with tissues to wipe away runny
mascara from her cheeks

at the next stop, a young man in a silky suede
suit steps on then sits across to intently stare at
her as shaky hands wring tissues dry as they fall
apart; touched, he walks up to her and hands her
an embroidered monogrammed handkerchief
    thank you, i appreciate this, but can't return
    it because i don't have your address

    no worry, i have more; my friends call me
max, short for maxine; if you like, i can walk you
home as i have nowhere else to go right now, my
business dinner is finished, and i'm free until
tomorrow morning

elliot m rubin

3 - 6 am

max, how do you like your coffee
    black   two sugars, please
after breakfast, they dress and walk to the
subway where they kiss before max leaves

one-night stands are not permanent romances,
like the tide ebbs and flows; occasionally, water
gathers on the beach in a dug-out hole to hold it
and prevent it from leaving

unfortunately, it didn't happen with emma
max disappeared into black underground tunnels
of the new york city subway system

forever

friends get together

the backyard bbq party's
pleasant enough
i really don't know all
my host's friends
although i probably met them
decades ago
when younger   at another home

smash burgers sizzle on the flattop grill
over onions basted
in organic irish grass-fed butter
while thick, sliced,
cheddar cheese squares, wait
until freshly baked browned buns crisp
then thrown on the meat

interesting small talk
with strangers until i see
susan walk in the house
without her husband, and robert follow
no one else notices
as i bite into a delicious cheeseburger
with sautéed onions and mesquite sauce

after a middling amount of time
they re-enter
her blouse slightly wrinkled
his shirt mis-buttoned
i open an ice-cold beer
from an over-filled cooler
later, i found out they used to date
before they married, others

elliot m rubin

sit by me
published May 2024 Juste Literary

the old wooden pier is peaceful
my legs hang
as cool mountain lake water
flows through toes
small sunfish scoot under
while listless, i watch
as a lone hawk
spreads magnificent wings
and circles the water
small birds hide in trees
which line the shoreline
like a waistband holding back a bloated dinner
the sun has passed noon
shadows float out from the shoreline
reaching, stretching, trying
to cover everything it can, and
eventually will
but i should be gone by then
building a fire encased by ancient stones
dug out when my home's foundation was formed,
and the underbrush
pruned back, trees cleared, land leveled
allows me to relax and
view humanity's vision of nature
when back on my old wooden dock

memories sit on the sofa with me

not one or two, but a lifetime collection
scooped up in a wide snow shovel
then dumped in my consciousness

the time i learned to drive a three-speed
manual transmission, on the column,
in a small nash-metropolitan car in brooklyn

helped me when my friend broke
his eyeglasses, and i drove him home
from rural new jersey to queens n.y.
over the george-washington bridge

in his low, tiny, red,
austin-healy sprite convertible
one summer night, wind blowing my hair, and
manhattan lit up in front of the windshield

an experience burnished in youth
senses aware and alive, everything noticed,
as big rig wheels sped past me
at eye level

elliot m rubin

transitions

the southern part
of manhattan's faux forest
filled with tall steel trees,
their balconies, modern branches,
overhang twisted paths
which snake through
greenwich village on
a cobblestone street
to irritate feet —
then you continue to stroll on
an undergrowth of concrete
where tribes of people gather, before
they go down dugout caves with
mechanical snakes to carry them
to outer-suburban pastures
filled with wood-built homes,
black, asphalt-stone driveways,
roads of green grass with no trees,
and miles of flattened former farm fields
with sprinklered wet lawns everywhere

bensonhurst brooklyn

the crowd gathers around
the exploded car
ambulances left in a hurried whirl
as sirens shriek —
on the ground
around the burned car's carcass
glass shards are embedded
in a pool of wet red blood;
a burned pair of woman's shoes
lay on the driver's side floor, while
on the sidewalk lie two listless bodies
of children, there is no chest movement;
they don't look peaceful
like hollywood movies make it seem —
i hear in the distance police cars and
ambulances who arrive to cover them
in cloth, then push everyone back,
this is no accident
    but a brooklyn mob farewell
to send a message the turf war has started —
the two passersby are collateral dead
on busy eighty-sixth street under the el
on a breezy fall afternoon
when a sidewalk filled with shoppers
learned tragically, it was the wrong car

elliot m rubin

a hippie date 1962

  pearls go with everything
as my date greets me
and when the door opens
she wears a longish
hand-strung single strand
of cream-colored iridescence
    and nothing else

she asks me in
before we go out
supposedly to discuss
the economic imperatives
in today's society
then closes the door
before she closes the deal

afterward
we don't go out
but order food in
exhausted
from playing in sin
according to church doctrine

i never meet with her again
tells me she only had a fling
to even up her husband's thing
now i know the meaning of   *to swing*

music at an arena

the rock concert sells out
a megastar from the shore
plays hit after hit
as the high seats are high
from hit after hit
of inhaled weed smoke
when clarence's sax
starts to wail
the arena goes crazy

everyone is on their feet
to sing along word for word
as a cloud of smoke
covers the stage, created by the audience
in a smoke-free building, all but ignored,
rolled marijuana cigarettes
lite up, people hit up,
coolness and calmness float,
peace, sex, rock and roll rule
      everyone's happy
it's a great happening concert
in the meadowlands tonight

elliot m rubin

he found out

she's a flea market girl
attractive
intriguing, and
thoroughly picked over

her wares exposed
for all to inspect
too often, it seems
for most who stop by

she has nothing new
everything shown
been extensively used
with reasonable prices

some even say
she's a cheap flea market girl
sells her stuff
where she stands every day

maybe that's why he likes her

business life

when i was younger
i walked
the thin, high trapeze of business
with no net below
only sawdust-covered hard ground
to welcome me six feet down
if i failed and slipped
people below sat in awe
half of them hoped i made it
the rest looked for a splat
to see my body squished flat
under my feet felt firm steel wire
stretched from one side
to the other, my challenge
was to succeed while others fell

if i made it
fame or fortune is mine
                          if not both
now almost eighty
mentally ready
again, for a high-wire act
my body resists
tired, troubled knees,
hand tremors from kidney disease
too ready to nap again midday
i sit with closed eyes
to dream what if

elliot m rubin

bergdorfs shoe department

elegant, the proper description
everything is more than adequate —
a doorman at the store entrance to
sofas where you sit to try on shoes;
a pair of satin slippers trimmed
with gold cording twisted around
the top of soft foam footwear
lay on a silk-lined sliver of a shelf—
women of a certain status shop here,
wealthy beyond belief, they float in
wave after wave to seek exclusivity
wont to be seen with the masses outside —
malaysian twelve-year-old girls
hand sew twisted gold cording
onto foam-soled silver slippers,
eat fish head soup from a common bowl
for lunch and dinner, and wear the
mis-weaves at work
or take them home

poems momma never read me

the marisol[1] sea

on tuesdays i visit my friend
her femininity is deep and blue
when i dip my toe in her charms
at first, she's cold and forbidding

once i acclimate to my marisol
she wraps her arms around me
envelopes me in her bodice   with
wave after wave of soothing charm

to lull me to feel safe –
i know better than to succumb
to her tantalizing, dangerous charms
as her pets are ravenous and deadly

no matter how enjoyable the entanglement
i embrace my lover at arm's length

---

[1] Marisol sounds like "mar y sol," Spanish for "sea and sun."

elliot m rubin

finished

when a poet dies
a part of humanity does, too
their personal meter expires

will the universe mourn the loss
who is going to continue
to write the unobvious
in words to entertain
not offend?

who will do it

stanzas need to be written
syllables counted
sonnets incubated
    in a mind's fallopian tubes
as they wait to be born

remember,
there's no time
without rhyme
for endings

ending

it's raining on his life
he's very wet, not drenched
soaked might be a better word

things didn't turn out as he thought
times could have been better
he was on track for greatness
but life,
like the universe,
is chaos;
even the gods sometimes struggle

at this point in life
the blackness entices
    although it's a definite future for everyone
he feels like rushing it

all depends how he feels
tomorrow
when he wakes up

elliot m rubin

bowling queen

knew her years ago
she was a saturday night fever girl
bleached blond
high teased hair
tight clothes painted on
unbuttoned to air out fuller cleavage

a great bowler in the alleys
used custom-drilled fingertip balls
she knocked down the guys
like bowling pins,
plenty of strikes, never strike out,
always made her spares dance

until one day
went with her boss
while he drove
she was busy doing her thing
when a taxi broadsided them
they say she bent over
to tie her sneakers and
neck snapped
too bad,
she was a good bowler
with the right ball in her hand

sapiosexual

those eyes
light blue grey
bleached blond hair
purple highlights
set above perfect lips
pink, pursed, ready
she's way above my level
a gym-ready body
trim and fit
washboard abs
with my aged body
i never expected a date

then she walks over to me
i really enjoy your books
usually loquacious
i stood silent
she took my hand in hers
my body warmed
skin melts off bones
immobilized
all i could do is smile
she asks me to dinner
it was our first date
those many years ago

elliot m rubin

jobs

everyone works
everyone does something
to earn money

except writers of poetry

poets live on love
though it doesn't pay
it is addictive
a mental high
with each written stanza

poets are the holy priests
of literacy
praised when read
usually,
after they're dead

barber shop

my daughter always cuts my hair
this time, her schedule prevents it
reviews for local cutters are pretty fair
i see young barbers who just stand there

cut, cut, clip, clip, scissors flash away
hair on the floor, do i go or do i stay
old men grayed all over sit and stare
thought of leaving, or stay, do i dare

i think i'm cool and way too hip
to be seen here or anywhere there
my uncut tresses i grew too long
will the cut be good, or probably wrong

all the barbers don't speak english
to be honest i am very skittish
how do i tell them only a trim
 it's too late now, so i recite a hymn

how can a short-haired poet write –
like samson, his strength took flight
no longer wordy; he looks like a nerd
great poems no more; they read like a turd

elliot m rubin

adventuress

she was different
not your idolized reader
or writer
life is to be used, abused, and lived
not to be buried with regrets
lovers, husbands, even a wife
never could fully understand her

a quench for life never achieved
or ever published
stacks of papers on the floor
each a diary of sorts
nobody read
until death came, then
friends and family finally found her

rural life

in the north country,
there's an old farm
run by an old couple
who had the land handed down
from one generation to the next
like siblings who hand-me-down clothes;
the old tree next to the barn, by the roadside,
now tilts, no longer straight and strong
the battles of winter storms weathered it
weary like the farmers,
it leans too often, too far,
only massive stakes and wires keep it up, and
not felled across the small road,
as cows stand under it for shade in heat,
in rain for cover,
and sheep graze about
impervious to the elements
while in the distance,
coyotes wait in the bush until mealtime,
when the sheepdogs go in for the night,
and only the largest one's left
to guard the flock with its life

elliot m rubin

thorns

broken hearts
can be fixed
it takes time and
understanding

cupid has a fistful of arrows
and waits for the right person

the rose garden's
filled with color
symbols of love and affection
superficial thorns overcome
by inner beauty and smiles

venus lives
in the thick thicket of romance
eager to embrace a broken heart

repairs can be made
love always seeks love

sleep

can't sleep through the night
awake at 3 am
to write poetry
until i notice
letters are blurry, and
thinking gets fuzzy and wuzzy
the solution to uninterrupted sleep
is a marijuana gummie

works every time
in the morning
restart with rhyme

elliot m rubin

migrants

the rabble, dressed in rags
soiled, slovenly, smelly
begs for food
on a park row corners
in a dickensian reality

the wealthy
in third-world countries
live lavish lives
in gated haciendas
with armed guards on patrol
and high-security wired walls

while miserable masses march
to a land of promise
if they can sneak in,
swim across a wide flowing river, or
walk across the dry, desiccated desert
helped by smugglers
who steal, rape, or abandon them

survivors surrender
to border guards
hope not to be returned
to the nation they fled

bayonne n.j. teardrop

it is polished to a reflective finish
as it hangs overlooking the harbor
waves crash onto the rocks below
and the new york city vista is in view —
after 911 the russian dictator gifted it
as a symbol of enduring friendship

now it cries for mother russia
the innocents who died due to his whims
now displayed on a former naval base
turned cruise terminal
where you can pass
huge passenger ships on your way
to the end of the road
to the end of the land
to the beginning of the sea
to find
a symbol of enduring friendship
from another era/error

elliot m rubin

early morning walk

dead bird on the ground
feathers abound
the red fox's stomach
now full and round

a 1950 sleepover

at grandma's home is exciting
never forgotten
i'm five
the antique wooden twin bed is too long
high off the ground
with white, wrinkle-free
starched stretched sheets
heavy blanket
soft down pillow

she lives on the second floor
over dad's store, while my window
faces coney island avenue and
steel trolly-car wheels below
grind loudly through the night
and car lights reflect
through pale translucent shades
crossing
from one side of the ceiling
to the other
while grandfather
in the bed next to mine,
after drinking a large milk glass of
martin's twenty-year-old scotch
snores too loudly for me to sleep
until
    i'm
      exhausted

elliot m rubin

in memory of

every year
every oscar's show
honors by name and picture
members who died
the crawl below their name
mentions a profession

everyone else in life
chisels in stone
what their departed was
mom, dad, son, daughter,
sometimes a platitude
sometimes a shameful reminder

death does not erase
nor ease deep anguish
it ends a lifetime
of either good or bad
it's that simple
it's that simple

hatred

where does it stop
here, there, hopefully somewhere
the insults, shouts, profanity
why   is the question

all mothers want their children
to live long
live happily
not end up malnourished
in a bombed-out desert city
starving
or killed by terrorists
after gang rapes
with women's breasts cut off
vaginas mutilated with nails

where is normalcy, decency
hatred kills both sides
when do we say enough?

elliot m rubin

public school butterfly

the caterpillar trudges along
slow, brown, a leafy diet
no one gives it a second glance
kids side-step to give it a chance

in school, she was a plain jane
nerdy and thin, not chosen to win
ate alone at the lunch table for years
every night, she'd read and stream tears

went off to beauty school to learn a trade
new friends taught her to glam up an image
emerged from her cocoon a fancy butterfly
men's heads now turn as she walks by

with confidence and strength, she'll fly
leave behind a ground-level youth
sunlight shines on spread colorful wings
majestic maturity attracts successful things

in memory of a friend

there are many gardens;
in a particular one i knew,
there was a tall, slender flower
it radiated warmth and kindness
it's stem stood steel straight
collected sunshine with
petals bright and lively
oozed with charisma
attracted people with laughter
until the florist in heaven
clipped it from its earthly vase
to brighten all the angel's days

elliot m rubin

retirement

absorbs thousands of footsteps
when the sun opens its arms
to allow warm rays to beat down
as we walk miles hand in hand

our love burnishes its imprint
on pounding hearts and implants
pheromones in brains, and brands
itself on our lives forever

in the distance, past the sand dunes
the soft sound of crashing waves
are sailboats on the horizon
as our legs tire, and we decide

to sit on a bench arm-in-arm, as you
place your head on my shoulder   yet once again

death of a sonneteer

rest in peace dear sonneteer
three quatrains and a couplet end
in iambic pentameter
with fourteen lines combined
in total   no more
rest in peace dear sonneteer
his quill and ink   now retired
rhyme and meter   to be forsaken

he forged ahead with modern prose
no longer needs to count ten toes
to stretch a near rhyme to slay its foes
rest in peace dear sonneteer
your rhyme scheme no longer speaks
of italian or shakespearian tongues
only now clearly written stanzas
with consonant rhyme and
clever interior ones   to stimulate
rest in peace dear sonneteer

elliot m rubin

newspapers

they are somewhat gone
from manhattan's printer's square
a reminder of a past era
where ben-franklin stands tall in bronze
the old herald-tribune building gone
replaced by a block-long university, and
the thin, slim, old new-york-times building
is still there, now repurposed —
the huge rolls of trucked canadian paper
waiting to be unraveled into pages
are a memory
as is the black printer-ink
darkened fingers
when i turn pages, now
banished and replaced
by digital screens
where you swipe left, right, or up
with washed fingers never soiled —
missed are the current obituaries
of friends and neighbors
with their lives condensed
into small inch or three-deep columns
never to be seen again
their deaths missed and assessed
until years later
when someone mentions it
or   never

city pizza shop

a small store on a small slip of stores
located in a busy business building
the corner pizza parlor is hectic
in and out, in and out, customers stream
and **gino** the manager will scream
next, wad'dya have buddy
                    cheese slice   yells back
the next one   *pepperoni please*
then, a lady dressed in blue
with three strings of fine pearls asks
for   *half sausage and half mushroom*

lunch time's hectic in midtown manhattan
anara is a new hire who makes the pie
it didn't hurt she caught gino's eye
her latina new yawk attitude and accent
blends in with the turmoil of the crowd
dust with flour, swing, and spread the dough
ladle the sauce, sprinkle with cheese
everything's rote by now, quick, quick, then bake
she doesn't walk more than four feet
yet does ten thousand steps each day
and tries to keep gino at bay some way
cause after hours the door locks,
lights out, they meet in the back room
to bake themselves some love

elliot m rubin

surprise!

first date
she's late
one drink
two drinks
up to four
or more
month from
first date
she's late

starstruck

you are my oxygen
together
we fuel a hot sun
as the world floats around us
our moons small and many
they split off into the vastness
as gravity loosens
         and they   float   away

   on their own

into the blackness
of the unknown
eventually
   our heat expires
and we join a galaxy
of related past stars
in nothingness

elliot m rubin

dawn

she wrapped her
twenty-five-year-old
petite arms
around a sixty-year-old neck,
pulled her black,
supple, soft, sexy skin
against an eager, white,
aged, sugar-daddy's body,
to whisper words
in his ear
lovers say to each other
as they entangle

wish more could be written
ecstasy's hard to describe
when you visit heaven
    then return home
to a white picket fence family
in a staid, suburban, station wagon
where on sunday
everyone attends church
to hear the choir praise the lord
with sermons on family values

today's world

the shining city on the hill
famous people speak of often
where fairness, equality, and
opportunity awaits
i have discovered
is only a mirage of hope

in my educated mind
a thought exists in reality
    but is an illusion
    in today's political world
where skin color matters
with fairness
bought behind closed doors
and law and order
is for the others
not them

elliot m rubin

simple joy

there is nothing better
on a hot summer day
when sunbeams scorch
with unbearable rays of
heat and stifling air
a torrential rainstorm
leaves mud puddles in fields
and a barefoot child
jumps and runs through
with splashes of cold,
brown, muddy water
to coat bare legs, as it
seeps between tiny toes
to mom's consternation
a bathtub eventually
is ringed with muddle residue;
another thing for her to clean

missing, 2024

where are the children
they're supposed to play outdoors
there are no giggles or laughter to be heard
it's a sunny day, and my window is washed
yet when i look out, they are missing

where are the children
millions of guns in america killed them
common sense solutions nowhere to be seen
because politicians have no empathy
for grieving parents
or spine to make useful laws

where are the children
who are buried
with politicians who offer
useless thoughts and prayers
as gun lobbies rake in cash
to a cold-hearted, gun-loving congress
while children continue
to be slaughtered

elliot m rubin

forbidden

the snow falls quietly on my yard
while i sit dry inside
reading the morning newspaper
on the 58th anniversary
of bloody sunday
on the edward pettus bridge;
though the paper's slightly wet
it's dry enough to read obituaries
    as old men tend to do
when moist, black ink
seeps onto my fingers
to remind me of a girl in high school
who sat with me every day at lunch;
i wanted to date her   but never did —
her smile was brighter than the sun, and
a warmth in her heart touched mine —
we could not socialize together privately,
although we came close,
but that error/era in social timelines
would not allow it

tennessee

the long drive to dollywood
is amazing
growing up in brooklyn   i never
imagined how big my country really is
the highways surrounded by thick-growth forests
and mountains that never stop rolling
through the middle of nowhere

as i approach chattanooga
the big band choo choo song sang in my head
until i turn off the interstate
to drive slowly
over a one-lane bridge
in the middle of nowhere

which let me enter pigeon forge —
suddenly i'm driving on local six-lanes
surrounded by motels
while tons of people wander about
as in las vegas   except it's
in the middle of nowhere

surrounded by the great
smoky mountains national park
this small town
is the honeymoon spot for
five contiguous states
in the middle of nowhere

elliot m rubin

sunny monday morning

weekend receipts in an envelope
cash, checks, correctly collated
i'm about to walk in first national bank
when cop cars converged
four feet from me
guns drawn
they run in the building
fearless
no alarms heard
silent   ones   mean   danger
people scatter
sidewalk clears
no need to wait
too much at stake
deposit hidden in $port jacket pocket
early enough
to visit another branch
just another
sunny monday morning
in brooklyn

long-lived

she had a good life
ups and downs
no different than others
loved and lost through the years
married twice
widowed twice
a bunch of kids
now grown
made a handful of good friends
outlived them
now in her late nineties

alone

sleeps all night
daytime too
is this a quality life
worth living

she now longs for death

elliot m rubin

breath[2]

i love you
he said with last breath
then quickly buried
upon his meth death

---

[2] The prompt was to use the word *breath* in a 15-word poem

led astray

his father
red, conservative
through and through
church and country
not the reverse
blames public education
for his son's liberal thoughts
in blue denim jeans
blue votes, and
wants freedom for all
but not narrow
antiquated beliefs
his dad professes
but the progeny
tries to keep the past past
to move liberty forward

a person's body
is their domain
red righteous politicians
have no right to be there
yet they say one thing
but when personally needed
do the opposite

elliot m rubin

another night of love

the hotel restaurant
is located in a side wing
in front of a small, hidden, elegant bar
filled with leather-lined booths
where quiet conversation occurs
and grainy, oiled walnut walls
keeps secrets that slips between lips
at midnight
over a whiskey mocktail cocktail
when a room key slides slowly across a table
under a small square natty napkin
as her hand gently covers his
then she brings the key back
into an open, gifted, camel-colored
louis vuitton pocketbook he gave her
with initials burnished on the left side
while the table's floral centerpiece
of red and yellow roses, with a green leaf filler,
starts to droop as the day ends, and
depression sets in when the room key opens
to the empty bed where her honeymoon started
years ago
now alone with her wealthy, elderly, overweight
sugar daddy coming any moment
for her to pay living expenses
since her beloved ended his life two years ago
due to a drug overdose in a roach and
rat-infested abandoned apartment in brooklyn
leaving her and two kids penniless

look back at life

once we were steel beams
rigid, strong, almost impervious,
built tall towers of accomplishments
as we plowed through life's roughage

like most things, time took its toll
we paid it in sweat and toil
our bodies no longer youthful
now bent, lean sometimes, i fall

tired eyes betray what we see
sometimes blurry or even unseen
canes and aids are present every day
never alone anymore when out the door

handsome trees and pretty flowers
fond memories beyond current abilities

elliot m rubin

success

what does it feel like
when you try to get ahead —
overnight bloomers
are hidden
as they struggle
to achieve
sometimes it takes years
to plan and do

my father and uncle
were prolific letter-writers
politicians of all persuasions
received their thoughts-
when my published books
reached number two on lists
i wish they were here

i want them to hold my books
to read my words
for loved ones to acknowledge it
but that will never happen
success feels good

but empty

misophonia,[3] a sonnet

there are some things people do
to drive a sane person crazy
like open mouths when they chew
it's hard to close two lips if lazy

munch, crunch, teeth scrunch
who wants to listen to you eat
i'd rather change my seat
and skip a delicious lunch

they eat like a horse
for everyone to be disgusted
not one bite of remorse
on a meal that's a five-course

chew your food with a closed mouth
no need to hear it before it goes south

---

[3] making noise to irritate others

elliot m rubin

poetry books

as you travel on a reader's poetic road
books roll down bookstore hills and
an obscure poet might catch your eye

most poetry tombs are filled with pebbles

occasionally, one book blocks the road
with a boulder of a poem
a reader can't ignore, forget, or go around

rarely, in a lifetime
a whole mountain cascades into
the roadblock book of poetry
readers will cherish for life

depression

they look normal
some handsome
some beautiful
most look like us
you and me
normal on the outside
but their insides stir wildly
sometimes, drugs and therapy help

they feel the world's worries
too intensely
too often

you can reason with them
until you run out of breath
their ears hear, yet
their mind is deaf
it's not their fault

they need to understand
the sun will still shine and glare
there is always a tomorrow
and someone does care

elliot m rubin

death wave

she stands at the foot
of the hospice hospital bed
looks at her brother
motionless
stretched out under three warmed blankets
plastic tubes keep him drugged and comfortable
his freight train
full of life experience
will shortly arrive at its final destination;
this is her time to say goodbye

suddenly, the fog of death dissipates
his eyes open with recognition
how long have you been here
i feel much better now
nurses walk-in
they quietly explain
he will be leaving us shortly

a near-death change is common
the stone pillar
of the family will soon crack and fall
the leftover pieces will be picked up
with heavy hearts
then put away forever

central park hawk cam

how they set the lens, i don't know,
but i watch the channel for hours
as a majestic bird puts on a show
it laid a few eggs in a rotted nest

high up in a fire-burnt tree
the thick branches stretch out
like a person yawning at awakening
tucked in a barked fold, a home of sticks

i see the hawk brought back by air
a young raccoon to feed her chicks
their ravenous appetite devours all
nature is cruel, with no regrets

next season i tune in again
more eggs are laid in the high up nest
when a mother raccoon climbs to visit
and eats the eggs, it's nature's revenge

elliot m rubin

food

every day a question asked
what to eat
when to eat
hot or cold
oh no
the bread has mold
guess it's now a choice of soups
she'll have the one with pasta loops
green-pea is the one for me
each sip a taste of glee
vegetarian mixed
with cubed breadcrumbed toast
which float around a turtle green moat
while my dinner's a well-cooked roast

beads

farm labor is hard and rough
calloused hands, life is tough
from dawn to yawn
they work the soil
earn small payment
for their toil
with small grain yields
they only eat peels
under harsh midday sun
they labor 'til done
the reward for hardy deeds
are buckets of tiny sweat beads
when buried and dead
their tombstones will have read
under this stone is a man alone
with nothing to show
for a life of work
but a bucket of sweat
he did not shirk

elliot m rubin

djt – the new york trial

heaven shined
angels rejoiced
a rainbow bestowed
its colors aglow
all was right
on earth below
as snakes slithered
away all-day
lambs munched
on a tasty grass lunch
while lilith in florida
left her indicted love
to wiggle and wrangle
in a potboiler legal hell
as new yorkers rejoiced
all is well
many prayed for this
it seems so swell
he'll trade his red tie
for stripes and a cell

snow buries everything

green grass of summer's
smothered roses,
lilies, lilacs gone
a colorful memory
of past season's blooms

the black asphalt
now white and impassable
only memories left
to meditate on

my love lies still
under a small grass-covered hill
soft snow gently falls
as winter's chill calls

her pure heart succumbed
to the stress
couldn't beat fast enough
now sleeps in her wedding dress

elliot m rubin

touch

a lithesome young blond smiles at me
dressed in jeans with dangling hoops
a blurry red devil tattoo on upper arm,
i see them as she stands on the station platform
while my train pulls slowly away
caught off guard, i wonder
why she flirts with me as i pass
i can't let it be

must talk and get her name, at least,
millions of unknown girls live here
this mystery to solve is going to be a beast

every day i stand at her stop
an hour before my train and
an hour past
when i know i should be on it
it's now a love challenge
must try to find her
if i can
because my heart was touched
with her smile

underwater

my parents
left me as an orphan
long before
the doom
of climate change knowledge —
now i need to deal with a future
when ice caps melt and
flush their contents
into the seas
lowlands flood everywhere

my buried family
always thirsty
due to diabetes and
kidney issues —
soon will be satiated
and never thirsty again

elliot m rubin

more time

we never know
about tomorrow

remember
mother's gentle embrace
it lingers
a lifetime in memory
  her scent,
  soft voice,
  advice,
  love hugs,
stays forever, enables
future generations
to grow with love
and empathy

if only
i had more time

nanny

last night
my friend's granny
died
distraught
he silently
cried

she raised him
when his mother passed
and the boyfriend left
to party forever
somewhere unknown
he didn't want to be a father

i told him
granny will be with him
at the next sunrise

he'll sense
her tender touch
when his skin
feels her warmth
every sunny morning

elliot m rubin

choose me

when i was a young boy
i dreamed i was a cowboy
hopalong was my hero
he wore black and
fought the bad guys
while he could shoot and
ride a horse galloping in a posse
eventually   i find out
it is only make-believe

as a teenager, war shows
on television enamored me
i thought of *west point*
the army as a career, then i find out
it's real blood and death

in my twenties, college
and girls were my agenda
while i date a beauty contest winner
who is a narcissist, i came
second after her needs, always
then realized
kindness and empathy
are more important

later in life, i understand things better
i need to choose myself to be a person
who seeks normalcy, decency and
leave the fantasy to others to live out

poems momma never read me

alone

hundreds surround her
yet no one speaks
lost in a sea of humanity
a city is a lonely place

a pretty girl's face
unnoticed
wave after wave of people
flow around her
as if an outcrop
on a jagged rocky shore

no one splashes hello
in her direction
absorbed
loneliness
in an ocean's metropolis of millions

elliot m rubin

hospital

an elderly husband walks in
the hospital one day
as the angel of death tags along
to take the man's last breath —
the undertaker wheels
him out zippered
in a black plastic bag
to whisk away on an overcast day
while the widow is bereft
of compassion for doctors
who neglected her husband
to try and cover up their oops, we goofed —
the insurance company paid her off
with a sizable check to help recover
as she basks in the acapulco sun,
drinks pina coladas on the beach
while her new, young, latino boyfriend
flexes his muscles
in a barely there string swimsuit
to amuse his sugar mommy
from america

poems momma never read me

key west morning

the summer sun shines through
a screened window
to dance on my sleepy eyelids
as salty ocean air
floats in my room,
all the way from cuba,
while on tree limbs
early birds tweet sweet songs
and six-fingered cats quietly watch
then silently extend claws
to climb for their breakfast, if lucky,
as i open the fridge
to take out three eggs,
olive oil to coat my pan,
while whole wheat bread toasts
and coffee pot percolates
with bubbles popping
in a clear glass top
to a rhythm
contra to the treed symphony
coming from outside

elliot m rubin

painful mornings

aches and pains come with age
gray hair thinned and tinted
not easy to reach older years
too many friends didn't make it

when i look in the mirror
i'm not there anymore
a stranger looks back at me

the tall, lean body of youth
now gone
he lives only in memories with old friends
and stories i tell grandchildren
at least those who will sit still and listen
while the younger ones play and roam
as i once did at my parent's home
those many years ago
in another world
far, far away in the past
no longer touchable

automotive people

people are a lot like cars
you can take them for a wash
clean off the exterior smudge mudge
till they sparkle clean and mean
yet it's not important how they look
it's what's under the hood that counts
the intent of their brain's horsepower
to do their part in humanity's path
with kindness and good intentions

elliot m rubin

they

protest war
rightly so
sit-ins, pickets, street blockades

they attack those who oppose them
property damage
violence
innocents hurt
police and ambulances appear
stun grenades, rubber bullets
real lead exits a gun-barrel
a body's hurt, dies

protests against war
bring death   not peace
protests bring violence home

they ignore the causes
see them through
one direction only with
dark, discriminating glasses

letter unsent

i wrote you a letter
then put it in a drawer
not sure
if i want to waste a stamp

you broke my heart

you, my soulmate, betrayed me
how can i continue this romance
when i know
what you did with our friend
    tried to hide it
    then a charge card statement came
you were to be far away
on serious business
    not monkey business
    in a local hotel
i called our friend on a hunch
who was away the same day
but when confronted
        she spilled the beans
my letter rages at you for cheating
    whenever this comes to mind
    i'll open the drawer   for a reminder
but i can't live without you

elliot m rubin

reflection on poetry

poetry is god's secret language
placed inside all he created
waits patiently, bides its time
until released to spread thoughts
in meter and rhyme
when it's prime
to soothe the soul
and stir the mind

monkey business

yabba yabba babble doo
most politicians only talk poo
election speeches are a wordy jumble
the voting season has become a jungle

he's going to solve all our problems
she's smart as a whip and will never slip
on issues slippery as a banana peel
you'll never see a smoky backroom deal

promises, promises, to everyone here
open your ears, and you will hear
everything your heart holds dear
it's the other side who throws a spear

once elected they never vote true
remember, it's you they'll willingly screw

elliot m rubin

big city stroll

when my friend deanna and i walk on essex
street, manhattan, we stop a moment at a pickle
store, then enter past open wooden oak barrels
rimmed with steel, filled way up with green
cukes, soaked in salt brine, to absorb spices,
garlic, and with no artificial preservatives, to
keep them cured for one to six months; the
barrels are filled with full-sours, half-sours, and
three-quarter sours too, where cucumbers
become a gourmet delight; then we grab a dozen
and take flight to katz's corner for a hand-cut
pastrami on rye sandwich you can die for; when
finished we walk down houston street to yonah
schimmel's knish bakery, where we purchase a
handful of freshly made potato knishes we intend
to bring home with us, but on the subway uptown
to pennsylvania station, we see sitting across
from us a mother and her three children, they
look hungry; deanna and i each give two of our
knishes to them, and we feel good, we did a
mitzvah, and we don't think our families will
mind after our full day on the lower east side of
the city

bad word

it's not a curse word
but can cause anguish
when good and bad
memories flashback
as it's said

if is a trigger word
if only i had said this or that
    maybe
if i tried more
we might still be together

if is a two-letter question
that can release
thousands of words
of regret and resignation

if
    we did something else
      we married a first amore
        we had loved more
          we complained less

if is such a powerful force
in a tiny, tiny word

elliot m rubin

camp gulag

a place where parents
are allowed to have fun
    elsewhere
while their spoiled rotten, undisciplined children
don't play sports, don't shower,
or eat wholesome gourmet meals

they sleep in non-air-conditioned tents
with dirt floors, old, smelly, bedbug
infested mattresses, and fire-hosed weekly
if the ~~wardens~~ counselors
think their body reeks too much

activities consist of sledgehammering rocks
digging in stone-infested trenches, then
fill them up using a small plastic beach shovel

meals of gruel are once a day
tiny pieces of protein float on top
if vermin are caught by campers
their entrails are added to the slop

camp gulag guarantees changes
upon their return home
    if not
there is a winter camp available
with un-insulated clothes
where they can freeze their attitude off

helper

lower manhattan streets
are narrow and curved
remnants of new amsterdam
in the day when dutch held sway
yet today
they gather flocks of harried walkers
who gawk at pretty people
on their way to work or lunch
while girls in short skirts
are fancy flowers at the front desk
employed by wealthy businessmen
who fly them to distant meetings
as secretaries
though they can't do shorthand or type
but their assets keep them at work
while they stay silent
to enjoy the perks of gourmet dinners,
lush hotels, and all-expense-paid travels
far from spousal questions

elliot m rubin

she's moving

after generations in the same house
overlooking lake champlain from vermont
the time came to sell and move
alone after her husband passed   her
eyes not what they once were
hearing barely functional   slight tremors
make error-free typing difficult

puzzled on how to say goodbye
to the old rose bushes she nurtured
hopes the local historical society
will care for them, and concerned for
a mother turtle who visits every season,
as a realtor arrives to write a contract
to start the process of closing
the genealogical door
while squirrels prance from tree to tree
they watch cars arrive and leave
in anticipation of a moving truck
to pack up past dreams and sorrows
in boxes   and bring them to a new residence
somewhere bland, with no history,
to mull about alone
in a newly painted new bedroom
for an old woman

thunderstorm

it's six in the morning
i hear the storm's heart
beat after beat
taps on my asphalt shingle roof
as pellets of rain
rush to slide off and
gush out forcefully
from semi-round tin gutters
onto welcoming, thirsty, spring, green grass
to saturate and nourish
the carpeted greenery around my house,
to enable my grandchildren
to run in mud; feel mother earth
ooze between tiny toes
on satiny tender young feet
as they squish down with giggles and glee
to bring bare skin in contact with muddy soil
as my ancient ancestors did eons ago
to leave small dinosaur-like
frozen footprints for future generations
to discover and wonder

elliot m rubin

rumor

there's no swirling wind outside
leaves still
temperature high
too humid to even breathe

yet sex did exist somewhere
when the nightly news announces
a rumored political scandal
of a thirteen-year-old girl
tied to a bed years ago
and raped by decades older
married man
who thinks this is okay
then told her afterward
you can always get an abortion

money buries the story
in a forgotten filing folder
in manhattan, as the
candidate continues
to proudly flout family values
holds up a bible for all to see
while the girl endures mental anguish
for years untreated
with justice blinded,

withheld, while life goes on

42nd street stroll 1963

the first thing i notice
on an iconic curb woman
are her long legs
enmeshed in black
skintight stockings
which hug snug alluring curves
like a second-skin

she always smiles
as i approach
a talk-to-me expression
then a solicitation
as a city boy
i've seen this implication
on too many corners
too many streets
they always ask me
if i want to do freaks
but i tell them honestly
  sorry, i'm on my way for some eats
they always reply
  too bad, I have something
  that nothing beats
  if you want some tasty treats
then i stop in **nedicks**
for a soda and hotdog
while she waits for dates
year-round, in heat or cold
not timid, always bold

elliot m rubin

music lovers

in high school,
i dated her
we both were in the orchestra
i played first bass fiddle
she played french horn;
sat directly in front of me
-

what enticed me
were her lips
pursed, muscular, sensual
the tiny muscle dot
on her upper mid lip
signified dedication

i'll never forget
her french horn lips
when we kissed
it was unlike any other

she had a mouth
that never died, or tired
i was exhausted
from being with her

right-wing politics

i stand alone
in a forest of rigidity

an isolated adult
with left-leaning liberal tendencies
as the world i once knew
no longer exists

education's stifled
with religious cult undertones
outside thoughts ignored
no matter how true
                shunted aside

in gerrymandered states
where can a person's intellect go
to fly free again

elliot m rubin

unnamed girl

she doesn't rise with the sun
  the sun shines when she rises
birds in their nest flutter wings
  clouds turn from grey to white
as she floats past high buildings
  on a wave of angelic love as
does romp in the woods below
  earthbound with their newborn fawns
while men sing her praises,
  vie for a smile to entice
the romance of their lifetime
  yet the key to her heart
is kindness and empathy
  and i miss her

directions

my car follows my heart
directions pre-mapped
follow the screen's line south
to visit florida's key west

lunch near hemingway's home
feel his soul and inspiration
in his small upstairs garage office
see a typewriter
which spit out his books
before anyone read them

i can't go to havana's el floridita bar
where he discovered his favorite drink,
daiquiris, with no sugar and double the rum

i'll have one
maybe two
then drink
his favorite brew

elliot m rubin

the universe is immense

too many stars to count
not enough fingers and toes
yet coincidence happens
without expectations

local obituaries in the paper
pictured an old lady
gray hair, facial creases,
though her name is bolded,
i did not know it,
below, her maiden name

i flash back sixty years
she was sixteen
i seventeen
one summer
we were hotter than a midday sun in july

cold of winter froze things
she lived in a different state
i did not drive

and it ended softly
in nothingness

skinny dipping in lake hopatcong, 1962

cavemen clubbed their women
conquered, then had their way
not like they do in society today

in the city you have to ask them out
a movie, then feed'em, still you wait
a few weeks pass for a sleepover date

for rural towns, far from suburban sprawl
in winter there's not much for kids to do
movies, bowling, then park in the dark

in hot july i'd date small-town girls, they
weren't prudes when they'd date their dudes
one summer week my folks drove back home

left alone with food and a landline phone
she came over one night to join for a swim
i had two beach towels, then jumped right in

we splashed and splashed, fish swam away
with moonlight, we dried, then began to play
later, dressed, content, she couldn't stay

lakeside summer homes are a teens delight
those happy years flew fast, then took flight

elliot m rubin

introspection

i am irreverent
irrelevant
possibly an irritant
to some
with irritating habits
that habitually hunts
the habitats of haunted hotels
looking for the ghosts
of past indiscretions

history

we made history
in our unique way
whatever we did
someone, somewhere
notices, or
will notice it, and

we'll be remembered for it
if not
it never happened

love's like that

elliot m rubin

peaceful neighborhood

after the first world war
rural america is vast
unsophisticated
every town has a village green
with a white bell tower church on one end
and city hall on the other
family homes with trimmed green lawns
white picket fences and
where tom, dick, jane, joan, and spot live
in a lovely era

after school jane and joan meet
behind the garage, out of view, out of earshot,
to experiment before adulthood
while dick would park his bike by jane's house
to collect cash the week's newspapers, he
delivers and her mother also pays him with an
experience while tom walks spot into the woods,
he loves spot dearly, maybe too dearly

tom's dad always helps jane's mom
with things to fix around her house, and
always made sure she is satisfied —
it's a peaceful neighborhood
full of love

i remember her

years ago
we smoked weed
made love endlessly
promised the other forever

sometimes i wonder
    why my forever
    is not with me

where did my love go
    to disappear
    vanish
    gone

fondly remembered
those many years ago
she went off
to seek fame and fortune

found myriad successes
four husbands
numerous liaisons

but lost a life of forever true love

elliot m rubin

stuck inside

my right leg fractured
in two places
i'm confined to a wheelchair;
going outside is not easy

the day is now overcast
i sit by the sliding glass door
and watch trees and bushes
sway with wind-blown gusts

the long security dowel down in the track
is on the other side, by the desk,
if standing, i could stretch down,
but in the wheelchair, i'd flounder out

  lightning flashes

the sky turns dark grey
like mousey footsteps in the attic
i hear a pitter-patter of drops
on my skylight until the storm
releases a torrent of rain

  thunder roars

a small ground-level tsunami
washes away all the tiny things
absentmindedly left outside
never realized, never needed

in grammar school

poetry was a dentist's chair
it extracts memory
to drill in my mind stanzas
without meaning, until

bukowshi birthed me
into the world of lines
where meaning was meant
and rhyme not worth a dime

i walked the city streets
side by side with o'hara
his observations written
of everyday people

emily taught me
grammar and end lines
with m dashes all over   and
unlike her   a conviction
to write understandable lines

ginsberg's beat poems
brings jazz to words
with social feeling
and disturb the old crusts

elliot m rubin

clubhouse stories - 1

in the back of the clubhouse on a
side street in queens, off the boulevard

one finger frankie sits quietly in there
at *fat cat matt's* chair and twirls his long hair

where the guys at nite meet, and greet to gamble
while they wait for the boss to ask for a favor

sad sal is an undertaker for missing guys
he buries people *one finger frankie* brings in

like *fat cat matt* who lost his wedding ring
in a big cash pot and still owed some stash

now *one finger frankie* sits in *fat cat matt's* chair
wears his gold pinkie ring and continues to stare

while *sad sal* buried *fat cat matt* in a deep coffin
under *zia-maria* in a brass box atop flowers

clubhouse stories - 2

party time gone, now only a yarn
dead *fat cat matt* would sponsor the night

he rented out girls for friends and guests
brought a whore or four in through a rear door

they'd sing and dance, then nakedly prance
from lap to lap with smiles and kisses

older guys made out like they were their mrs
went with them upstairs to *sister maria's* rooms

who once was in a convent but forced to leave
they found her in bed with the *gardener steve*

she runs a chicken farm with very young hens
charges for roosters with a passion to cleanse

their bodies of inner energy and turmoil
they also kill to relax and bury in soil

elliot m rubin

clubhouse stories - 3

police sirens sound as loudspeakers blare
evacuate, evacuate; there's a gas leak *where?*

the whole block closed-off; electricity shut down
gas-masked men flood through a club's open door

the building's now empty, utility men inside
small microphones placed, they then try to hide

only f.b.i. knows who hangs out in the club
they'll record everything, hope some guy will flub

brag about jobs, police still did not solve
with bail, someday, they'll be out and revolve

back to old habits with crime waves to earn
till locked up for good, seems they'll never learn

About the Author

elliot m rubin is an exciting american poet who has been in numerous anthologies and books of poems. His free verse style of writing is refreshing and easily understood.

elliot m rubin

Thank you for reading this collection.

If you are interested in the author's other books, his website is:

www.CreativeFiction.net

_____

Also, please *follow* him on Instagram at

elliot_m_rubin
people poems